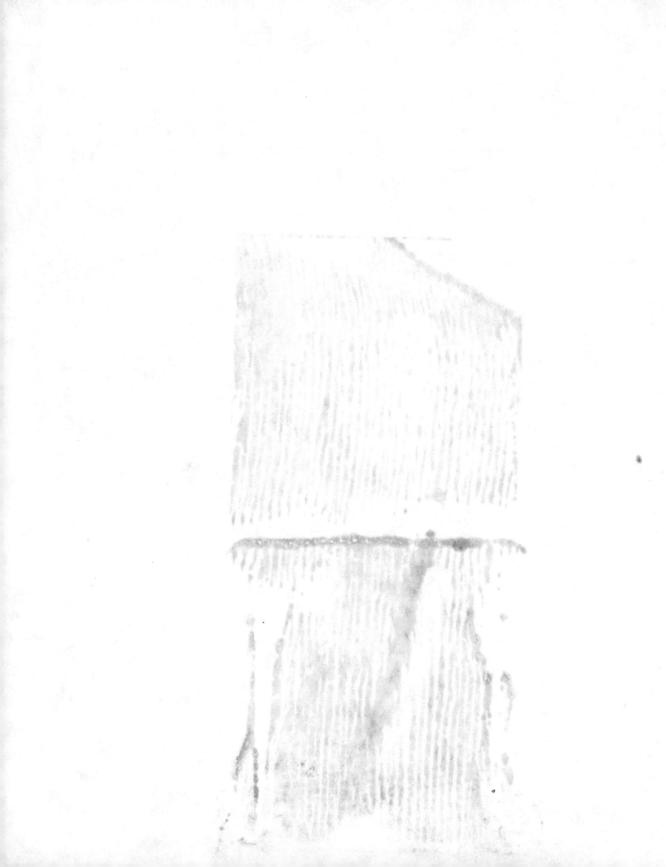

Science in Ancient Rome

XCVI

Jacqueline L. Harris

III

North
Sea

BRITAIN

ATLANTIC
OCEAN

E U R O P E

GAUL

SPAIN

ITALY

GREECE

Black Sea

TURKEY

Mediterranean Sea

ARABIA

EGYPT

Red Sea

A F R I C A

ASIA

N

0   750 km
0   500 mi

Science in Ancient Rome

XCVI

Jacqueline L. Harris

Science of the Past

FRANKLIN WATTS

A Division of Grolier Publishing
New York • London • Hong Kong • Sydney
Danbury, Connecticut

Photographs ©: Ronald Sheridan/Ancient Art & Architecture Collection, Ltd.: 15, 26, 30, 33, 36, 50, 51; Archive Photos: 17, 49; Art Resource: 19 (Erich Lessing), 16, 23, 24, 32, 41, 53, 54 (Scala), 56 (SEF) 11; Corbis-Bettmann: 12; e.t. archive: 27 (National Archaeological Museum, Aquileia) 18; Hulton Getty Picture Collection/Tony Stone Images: 58; Library of Medicine: 42, 55; Melissa Stewart: 20; Photo Researchers: 14 (Hubertus Kanus), 48 (John Sanford/SPL), 34 (SPL); Science Museum/Science & Society Picture Library: 38, 39; Superstock, Inc.: 57 (Courtesy of the Board of Trustees of The Victoria & Albert Museum, London/Bridgeman Art Library, London), 37 (Museo Capitolino, Rome/Canali PhotoBank, Milan), 43 (Museum of History of Medicine, Rome, Canali PhotoBank, Milan), 8 (National Historic Museum, Bucharest, Romania/ET Archive, London), 21, 44; Tony Stone Images: cover (A & L Sinibaldi), 6 (Glen Allison), 13, 25 (Paul Chesley), 46 (John Lund), 40 (Rod Planck), 10.

Illustrations by Drew Brook Cormack Associates. Map created by XNR Productions Inc.

Library of Congress Cataloging-in-Publication Data
Harris, Jacqueline L.
      Science in ancient Rome / Jacqueline L. Harris. —Rev. ed.
         p. cm. — (Science of the past)
      Includes bibliographical references and index.
      Summary: Describes how the Romans put to use and expanded the scientific achievements of earlier civilizations.
      ISBN 0-531-20354-9 (lib. bdg.)   0-531-15916-7 (pbk.)
      1. Science—Rome—History—Juvenile literature. 2. Science, Ancient—Juvenile literature. 3. Rome-History-Juvenile literature. [1. Science-Rome-History. 2. Science, Ancient. 3. Rome—Civilization.] I. Title. II. Series.
Q127.R58H377 1998
509.37-dc21   97-1901
                                                                                                          CIP
                                                                                                          AC

CONTENTS

chapter 1
The Romans Put Science to Work

Early Romans thought that lightning, volcanic eruptions, and other acts of nature were controlled by gods.

About 2,800 years ago, the sky suddenly grew dark over the village of Veii in what is now central Italy. A few moments later, rain poured down and jagged streaks of lightning began to flicker from cloud to ground. Huddling in their grass-thatched homes, the people watched.

"Don't be afraid," said a wise old man. "The lightning comes from the east—from the hand of the god Tinia. It is a good sign." The people smiled and sighed with relief. Tinia, the king of the gods who lived in the northeastern skies, was pleased.

The small village was in a country called Etruria. The people who lived there were called Etruscans. Their culture was the first *civilization* in Italy. The Etruscans eventually conquered the Latins and turned a small river village into the mighty city of Rome.

The Etruscans believed that natural phenomena such as lightning were messages from the gods. Their view of the world was very different from the one we have today. When we see lightning, we ask "What natural events caused this to happen?" The Etruscans wondered, "What are the gods trying to tell us? Have we done something wrong?"

The word "science" is derived from the Latin word "scientia," which means "knowledge." Science is a search for facts. We learn scientific principles by observing and studying the world around us. The Etruscans were not scientists because their way of looking at the world was based on superstition, not fact.

This photo shows a portion of an immense column that was carved about 2,100 years ago. It depicts Roman soldiers and workers constructing a building.

Some ancient peoples, such as the Greeks, were true scientists. They studied the world around them, recorded their observations, thought about their findings, and developed theories. Sometimes the Greeks tested their theories to see if they were correct. This scientific process helped them understand the world and the heavens.

The Romans, on the other hand, did not perform many experiments and made few scientific discoveries. What they did do is gather scientific knowledge from other cultures and use it to improve their lives.

The Romans were people of action—doers, rather than thinkers. They planned and built great cities. They developed new uses for metals, stone, and cement. Powerful Roman armies conquered all of Italy and then moved across most of Europe and into parts of Asia and Africa. By about 2,150 years ago, all the lands bordering the Mediterranean Sea were ruled by Rome. The city became a prosperous world capital and the center of Western civilization.

Wealthy and educated people from all over the Roman Empire traveled to Rome. These people brought ideas and information from their own cultures, and Romans found practical ways to use the information.

A Culture with no Scientific Vision

Most ancient Romans believed that duty and practical achievements were very important. They did not study or investigate the world just for the sake of learning. They thought knowledge that had no obvious practical use was unimportant.

For example, the Romans had no interest in mathematical theory. They spent their time developing ways to use the mathematical knowledge of other cultures to build great buildings. They learned nothing new about astronomy, but they did use what the Greeks had learned to make a more accurate calendar. They never thought to study the structure or function of plants. Instead, they combined plants to create "magical" potions. They believed that the gods controlled their health, the world around them, and the stars in the sky, so there was no point in trying to understand medicine, biology, or astronomy.

The Romans never realized that some of their inventions could have helped science advance. Although they understood optics, they didn't try to build microscopes or telescopes. Roman glassmakers built the first magnifying glass, but never saw its potential. They had no interest in observing the tiny organisms that lived all around them.

chapter 2

What Roman Builders Accomplished

The Colosseum was the largest arena
in the world until 1914.

Many of ancient Rome's greatest structures are still standing today. Structures such as bridges, sports arenas, places of worship, water delivery systems, and a great highway give us clues about what life was like for people who lived thousands of years ago.

More than 2,400 years ago, Roman engineers built a bridge called Ponte Milvio across the Tiber River. In its early days, the bridge was used by Roman soldiers marching off to war.

Ponte Milvio has stood the test of time.

A gladiator receives a thumbs down signal from the crowd, indicating that he should kill his opponent.

Not far from Ponte Milvio stands the Colosseum, an amphitheater built more than 2,000 years ago as an arena for Roman games. For the next 400 years, it was the site of contests between gladiators, battles between men and wild beasts, chariot races, and other types of public entertainment. The structure's marble and wood benches could seat about 50,000 spectators.

The Colosseum was made of brick and *concrete* covered with stone. About 1,200 years ago some of the stones were removed from the structure and used to construct other buildings, but the Colosseum's grandeur is still evident today. The first three stories of the Colosseum consist of rows of elegant arches. The fourth story, which was added later, is less decorated.

In the center of Rome stands the Pantheon, an ancient temple to the gods. The word "pantheon" comes from the Greek word "pantheion," which means "place for all gods." The structure was completed about 1,900 years ago. Like the Colosseum, it is made of brick and concrete. An

Light enters the inside of the Pantheon through an oculus at the top of the dome.

The Pont du Gard aqueduct, which was built by the ancient Romans, still stands today.

oculus, or opening, at the top of the dome-shaped ceiling lights the entire building. The portico, or porch, at the building's entrance is supported by eight massive columns. Many of the engineering techniques developed to build the Pantheon are still used today.

A trail of broken arches stretches over the hills and across the valleys surrounding Rome. These are the remains of *aqueducts*, channels that carried fresh spring water to the people of Rome. By the year 100, aqueducts carried 85 million gallons (322 million l) of water into the city each day. One famous Roman aqueduct, the Pont du Gard, still stands today. This aqueduct, which is located near Nîmes, France, is three stories tall and has a channel at the top. Roman engineers used stone, brick, or pozzolanna to build aqueducts. Pozzolanna is a mixture of limestone and volcanic dust.

One of early Rome's greatest architectural accomplishments was the Appian Way, the first and most famous military highway. The Appian Way is named for Appius Claudius Caecus, the Roman official who began the highway's construction more than 2,300 years ago. The road, which is still used today, originally extended from Rome to Capua. It now goes all the way to Brindisi, which is on the coast of the Adriatic Sea.

All of these structures were built using a few simple tools and a lot of hard labor. Many of the basic architectural ideas and techniques were borrowed from the Greeks and adapted to fit Roman needs. The Romans understood the importance of arches and used them to build aqueducts, bridges, and large ampitheaters. They also improved concrete, which was invented by the Egyptians, making a substance that was as hard as natural rock.

Although some parts of the Appian Way are more than 2,300 years old, it is still used today.

Arches were the most important elements of ancient Roman structures. They were used to support the windows and doors of buildings such as the Basilica of Maxenthius.

Roman Arches and Concrete

An arch may seem to be nothing more than a beautiful decoration, but it is actually an ideal way to support weight over long distances. Before the invention of the steel girders used to support today's skyscrapers, arches were the best way to strengthen a structure.

The arch was conceived by the Egyptians and Greeks. They discovered that wedge-shaped stones formed into an arch held each other in place. The Etruscans, and later the Romans, used this half-circle shape to provide support over doors and windows. They found that an arch is stronger than a straight support. But only when the Romans began to develop and improve the arch was its true strength discovered. Roman engineers learned that a properly designed arch could support bridges and aqueducts. A series of arches could support enormous domed ceilings.

Once Roman builders had a way of supporting huge weights, they needed a strong building material. That is just what they developed around 2,200 years ago.

From Egyptian texts, Romans learned that they could create concrete by adding water to powdered lime. When sand and stone were added, the concrete became stronger. And when Romans added volcanic ash from a site near Mount Vesuvius in southwestern Italy, the resulting concrete was even harder. Now the Romans had everything they needed to become master engineers.

Bridges and Aqueducts

When the Romans tried to build bridges across very wide rivers, they began to run into problems. Each concrete arch was supported by large square piers built into

The Romans used huge arches to support the weight of bridges. This bridge was built in Merida, Spain, about 2,100 years ago.

At one time, this aqueduct transported water to Istanbul, Turkey.

the riverbed. A wider river required more arches, and more arches meant more piers. Unfortunately, as more piers were added, water flow was obstructed and the water's force increased. As a result, the water began to scrape up large quantities of sand and gravel from the river bottom. This weakened the piers' attachment to the riverbed.

To solve this problem, the Romans began using larger arches. Larger arches meant fewer piers and less obstruction of water flow. Less material was scraped from the bottom of the river, so the bridge's support system was not threatened. The Romans built a number of very large bridges over major rivers in Spain using enormous arches. Many of these bridges are still standing today.

Adapting what they had learned from building bridges, the Romans built huge concrete aqueducts. These channels, which were supported by tall arches, carried fresh spring water from streams in the Apennine Mountains to Rome—a distance of about 15 miles (24 km). As the Roman Empire grew, Roman engineers built aqueducts to supply water to cities in Spain, North Africa, and Greece.

Once the water reached the city, it was stored in holding tanks. Any sand or small rocks that had been swept along by the water settled to the bottom of the tank. A system of lead or clay pipes carried the water from the holding tank to the fountains, baths, and factories. Wealthy people had water piped into their homes, but most Romans got their water from public fountains.

Lead pipes like this one carried drinking water to the homes of wealthy Romans.

Some of the baths built by the ancient Romans in Bath, England, are still in use today.

Public Baths

The abundance of water supplied by the aqueducts gave Roman builders an idea: Why not build public baths? Over time, these baths developed into social centers and saunas. In many cases, exercise rooms, game rooms, gardens, and libraries were added. These baths could be compared to modern health spas.

By the year 100, there were several hundred public baths in Rome. One of the largest, the Baths of Caracalla, was built in 212. It was bigger than twenty football fields and more than 1,600 people could bathe there at one time. Some of the most famous Roman baths were built in the city of Bath, England. The area has warm springs and mineral waters, which were believed to restore health.

Building a Highway System

Roman roads were so well built that they were sometimes called "walls lying on their sides." Most roads were constructed of four or five layers of sand, gravel, cement, and stone. They were at least 4 feet (1.2 m) thick—four times as thick as our modern highways—and 6 to 20 feet (2 to 6 m) wide. Although Roman roads were built mainly to move soldiers from one place to another quickly, they were also used by the government postal service and travelers. Travel centers located along Roman highways provided people with maps and information about local inns.

This ancient Roman road is known as Ostia Antica.

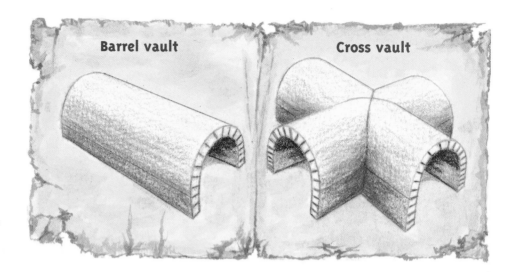

Barrel vault   Cross vault

The Romans used arches to build strong ceilings. A cross vault was especially useful because it allowed sunlight to enter the building.

Arched Roofs and Ceilings

The Greeks used massive columns to support the roofs of their large buildings. Other ancient civilizations used huge wooden timbers that often cluttered the interior of the buildings. The Romans came up with a better solution. They used arches.

When a row of arches is put together, one behind the other, the resulting structure can support an enormous amount of weight. The Romans called this type of ceiling a *barrel vault* because they thought it looked like a barrel that had been cut in half. It is also called a tunnel vault.

The one disadvantage of a barrel vault is that it requires thick supporting walls. As a result, there is no way for natural light to enter the building. The Romans solved this problem by inventing the *cross vault* (also called the

This gallery inside the Colosseum
has a barrel-vaulted ceiling.

The cross-vaulted ceiling of the great hall of the Market of Trajan lets in plenty of natural light.

groin vault). A cross vault consists of two barrel vaults that intersect at right angles. The result is a large square-roofed building that lets in plenty of light.

Some of the grandest Roman buildings had huge domed ceilings. A dome is designed by rotating a series of arches around a circular wall. The arches meet at their highest point. The dome of the Pantheon, which is made of brick and concrete, is more than 142 feet (43 m) in diameter. As Roman architects built their arches and domes, a new and beautiful city emerged.

The Pantheon has one of the most
impressive domed ceilings in the world.

chapter 3
Using Earth's Resources

These iron pruning knives were used
by Roman farmers to cut vines.

While scientists in other ancient cultures studied the world around them, the Romans searched for ways to use Earth's resources to improve their lives. They developed methods for growing healthier crops, purifying materials taken out of the ground, and making stronger metals.

Magical Manure

Early Roman farmers noticed that fields grazed by sheep, horses, and cattle produced the largest crops of rye and wheat. They realized that the animals' manure was enriching the soil. The nutrients from the manure were then absorbed by the plants. The Romans experimented with many different types of manure, and found that pigeon and chicken dung worked best. This was the beginning of the modern fertilizer industry.

Farmers who had no animals dug pits in the ground and threw in all kinds of waste—household garbage, dead plants, leaves, straw, and ashes.

Marble relief of Roman farmers plowing a field with oxen

Compost in a Bag

You can make your own compost to nourish plants in or around your home. If you live in a house with a large yard, you could try making a compost pile large enough to fertilize shrubs, a flower garden, or a vegetable garden.

1. Place 1 cup of *organic* waste, such as carrot or potato peelings, eggshells, coffee grounds, tea leaves, orange peels, banana skins, apple cores, grass clippings, leaves, or wood ashes in a large water-tight, self-sealing plastic bag.* You will get better results if the wastes are cut or chopped into very small pieces.

2. Add ½ cup (120 ml) of garden soil. (Do not use sterile potting soil.) Garden soil contains microorganisms that break down the wastes into compost. Stir in 1 tablespoon (15 ml) of alfalfa meal or alfalfa pellets (such as Litter Green cat-box filler or rabbit or hamster food). Pour in 1 ounce (30 ml) of water and seal the bag. Shake the bag well to mix all the contents.

3. Store the bag on a kitchen shelf. Every day, squeeze the bag a few times to mix the contents. Open the bag to let air in every other day. If the contents of the bag smell when you open it, they may be too wet or in need of additional mixing. After 4 to 6 weeks, your compost will be ready to use as fertilizer.

---

* Do not put any meat in your compost.

Every now and then the farmer would stir up this *compost* with an oak stake that had been driven into the center of the pile. As the waste material decayed, it too became excellent fertilizer.

The Romans also knew that certain plants—beans, clover, and alfalfa—seemed to enrich the soil. Today we know that these plants convert a substance called *nitrogen* into a form that all plants can use. Farmers would plant a field with wheat or rye one year and then plant beans or alfalfa the following year. This technique, called crop rotation, gave the soil a chance to replenish itself.

Treasures from the Earth

When the Etruscans settled in the hills of northern Italy about 2,900 years ago, they discovered that the area was rich in iron, zinc, tin, and copper. They knew the value of these metals and began to mine them.

At that time, miners dug shallow trenches along the ground and separated the metals from the soil. They had only the simplest tools—picks, spades, and hammers made of iron and wedges made of deer horns.

When the metal deposits, or *ore*, on the surface ran out, the miners dug deeper. First they dug a series of pits 50 feet (15 m) deep and connected the pits with tunnels dug underground. Then they removed the ore from the tunnel walls.

Copper

Because copper ore is especially hard, early Romans often had trouble mining it with iron tools. Luckily, they developed a very clever technique

A coppersmith's
workshop

for removing copper ore from surrounding rock. First, they built fires against the rocky ore bed. When the rock was very hot, the miners threw water against it. The rock shattered and the miners could select the pieces that contained copper ore.

After metal ores were removed from the ground, they had to be sorted, crushed, and washed. Most of the time the metals had to be separated from rocky impurities. Copper ore was *smelted*, or purified, in a very hot fire. These fires were built in large pits lined with clay. When the fire was hot, workers added ore and more wood to the fire, and covered the pit with clay. The impurities were burned away, leaving pure copper.

Gold

Roman miners also developed a special method for mining gold. First, they dug tunnels beneath a mountain until the entire mountain collapsed. Then they diverted a large mountain stream through a ditch dug across the top of the collapsed mountain. A small plant called gorse was planted along this ditch. As water from the stream flowed down the mountain, it picked up bits of dirt and gold. Small pieces of gold were then caught in the gorse and later removed by the miners.

Roman metalworkers crushed the small chunks of ore and mixed them with mercury, the only metal that is a liquid at room temperature. When the mixture was heated, the mercury and impurities boiled off, leaving pure gold. The Romans developed similar methods for purifying silver.

Making Metals Stronger

Roman purification techniques show that they understood basic chemistry and knew how to take advantage of the chemical properties of metals. This knowledge came from *alchemists*, the first chemists. Alchemists in ancient China and other parts of the world searched for magic potions that could make people live forever. They also wanted to change ordinary metals into gold.

Although alchemists were never able to accomplish their goals, they made a number of important discoveries. They found that if they mixed just the right amounts of copper and tin, they could make a dull, gold-colored material. This material, which we call bronze, is harder than

This bronze Roman helmet has scenes depicting the conquest of Troy.

32

either copper or zinc. The Romans used bronze to make strong swords, spears, and shields. The alchemists also made brass by mixing copper and zinc. Brass, a shiny, gold-colored metal, is easier to work with and more attractive than bronze. Brass was used to make coins, decorative cups and plates, as well as dress armor and helmets.

Refined or purified iron was not a strong or useful metal. But alchemists discovered that when red hot iron was hammered over a charcoal fire and then plunged into cold water, the result was steel. Steel is so strong that it is used today to support the world's tallest skyscrapers.

Although the Romans are not credited with discovering how to make steel from iron, they were the first civilization to see its potential. The steel sword became Rome's secret weapon. Using weapons of steel, Roman armies gained control of most of Europe, northern Africa, and parts of Asia.

A gladiator's knife made of iron, ivory, and bone

chapter 4
Healing the Sick

The Greek physician Hippocrates is considered the father of medicine.

"Drink cabbage juice!" "Eat goat fat!" This is about all the medical advice available to the sick in ancient Rome. The Romans believed that the gods caused illness. People could not prevent or control disease, so there was no point in studying it. Meanwhile in Greece, medicine was taking its first fumbling steps as a science. The Greeks were trying to identify the causes of diseases and find ways to cure them.

When the Roman armies conquered Greece about 2,300 years ago, they learned about Greek medicine. Most Romans did not approve of the way Greeks viewed disease. For example, Marcus Cato, a Roman general and leader who was opposed to the influence of Greece, wrote, "Whenever that nation [Greece] shall bestow its literature upon us, it will corrupt everything and all the sooner if it sends its physicians here. They have conspired among themselves to murder all foreigners with their medicine."

Greek Physicians Come to Rome

Some Romans disagreed with Cato. They invited Greek physicians, or medical doctors, to come to Rome and treat them. Archagathos was one of the first Greek physicians to practice in Rome. He quickly became famous as a healer of wounds. The grateful Romans allowed Archagathos to become a citizen. However, because he often cut his patients recklessly, he soon became known as the Carnifex, which means "the butcher."

This relief shows the Greek physician Asclepiades treating a patient.

Asclepiades, a teacher and public speaker, came to Rome about 2,100 years ago. One day, while speaking to a group of people on the street, he saw a funeral procession passing by. Something about the body made him think that the person was not really dead. Sure enough, a little massage and cold water restored the person to consciousness. Asclepiades' fame as a physician who could achieve remarkable cures quickly spread throughout Rome.

Later, Asclepiades developed a theory of illness. He thought that the body is made of tiny particles. A person becomes sick, he said, when these particles are not properly arranged. A person could be healed by reestablishing the particles' proper order. Asclepiades recommended that his patients get plenty of sunshine and exercise. He also advised them to take cold baths, drink plenty of liquids, and eat a special diet.

A bust of Asclepiades

Asclepiades was the first doctor to understand the difference between acute mental illnesses, which last for only a short time, and chronic mental illnesses, which last a long time. He treated his patients gently and calmed them with herbs, music, and sunshine. Asclepiades found that many of his patients could not pay attention or remember things, so he devised exercises to help them with these problems. This approach was quite different from the cruel treatment mentally ill patients had previously received. In many cases, they had been considered outcasts and were locked up in dark cellars.

Asclepiades's ideas were recorded by Celsus. He described the famous healer's theories about treating disease. Because this book was rediscovered in Florence around 1400, European physicians were able to learn from Asclepiades's experiences. Many of his treatment regimens are still used today.

Medicine Is Accepted in Rome

The successes of Asclepiades led Romans to think that some illnesses could be cured. Many healers learned surgical skills, and more than 200 surgical instruments, or tools, were developed.

Physicians also learned to set broken bones, and developed ways to remove tumors and other growths. They found that removing infected tonsils could help sore throats and realized that it was possible to save a patient's life by *amputating* an infected arm or leg.

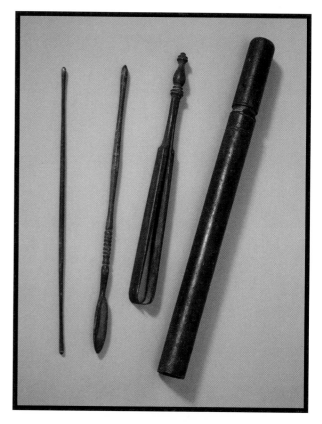

These Roman surgical instruments were made and used about 1,900 years ago.

Surgeons were especially successful in treating *cataracts*, a condition that clouds the lens of the eye and, untreated, can lead to blindness. Using a sharp needle, they gently removed the cloudy lens from the eyeball, allowing the patient to see much more clearly.

Meanwhile, Roman leaders began to recognize that they had a responsibility to protect the health of the people. Public medical service was available for everyone, even the poorest citizens. Roman officials also created a testing and licensing system to make sure that doctors were properly qualified to practice medicine.

Hospitals in ancient Rome were similar to our hospitals today. They had wards where patients were treated, kitchens where meals were prepared for the patients and staff, dining rooms where food was served to the staff, and apothecaries where medications were prepared. The idea of a public hospital is considered Rome's greatest contribution to medicine.

Painting of a Roman field hospital

Stopping the Spread of Disease

Although the Romans did not really understand how infections spread from one person to another, they developed a number of ways to stop viruses, bacteria, and other disease-causing organisms from spreading.

Rulers passed laws stating that dead people must be buried outside the city, and people who developed highly *contagious* diseases, such as *leprosy*, must move to isolated areas. The Romans knew that there is a connection between swampy land and a deadly disease that causes shaking and a very high fever. Today we know that this disease, *malaria*, is spread by mosquitoes, which breed in areas with stagnant water.

Some types of mosquitoes infect humans with malaria.

The Cloaca Maxima, the world's first sewer system, is still used to transport waste out of Rome.

About 2,500 years ago, Roman engineers built a trench lined with stone to drain a wetland near the city. Eventually, this trench was enlarged and extended through the main streets of Rome and flowed into the Tiber River. The top of the trench was enclosed by a barrel vault. The Romans dumped waste into this trench and public toilets were connected. This trench, which is now called the Cloaca Maxima, became the world's first major sewer system.

The Romans built sewer systems in all of the Empire's major cities. They knew that removing wastes cut down on the spread of diseases.

The Romans also knew the importance of eating fresh food and drinking pure water. Roman officials routinely inspected the food sold in markets. If they found spoiled fruit or meat, they removed it. Officials also checked the quality of water transported by aqueducts.

How the Body Works

While Roman doctors suggested remedies for patients with minor complaints and surgeons performed operations to solve more serious problems, other physicians studied the way the body's organ systems interact.

Rufus, a Greek from Ephesus, realized that the heart's beating moves blood through our *arteries*—blood vessels that carry the blood away from the heart. He was also able to determine which nerves move our muscles and which control our sense of touch. He also discovered that a fever is part of the body's effort to kill disease germs. Rufus's texts on *anatomy* and disease were later used by Arab physicians.

Aretaeus studied a variety of illnesses and wrote seveal books. If a Roman physician was not sure how to treat a patient, he could look through Aretaeus's writings for help. Aretaeus described the symptoms of dis-

Aretaeus studied the lungs, nerves, liver, heart, and brain. He was the first physician to describe diabetes.

A midwife assisting a woman who is about to give birth

eases that affected the lungs, the nerves, the liver, the heart, and the brain. He was the first to describe *diabetes*, a disease that results when the body fails to use sugar properly.

In *Apollonius' Commentary*, the author describes the treatment of bone dislocations and provides helpful drawings. This document was used by physicians for thousands of years. Another physician, Soranus, spent his time studying childbirth. In his book, *On Diseases of Women*, he advised women about delivering babies and caring for them after birth. He also devised special instruments to use when delivering babies.

Despite all the knowledge gained by Rufus, Aretaeus, Apollonius, and Soranus, many diseases puzzled Roman physicians. At about the same time, a healer named Galen came to Rome. Galen, who was well trained in Greek medicine and science, had a great talent for *diagnosing* and treating medical conditions. His ability caught the attention of Roman leaders when he cured the wife of an important official and successfully treated a famous philosopher.

A Medical Leader

Galen was confident that he could cure any medical condition. "I alone have indicated the true methods of treating diseases," he wrote. The Romans considered him a medical genius. Emperors and senators called

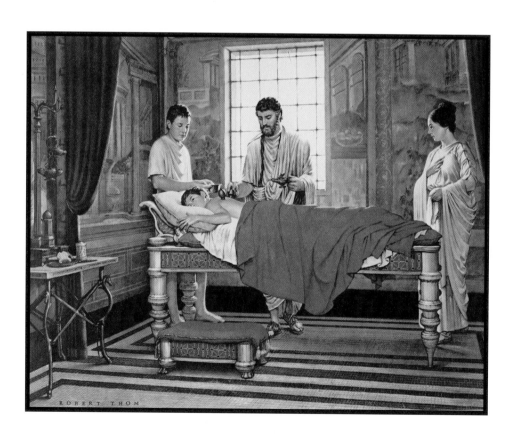

Galen treating a patient

him to their sickbeds, and his medical lectures drew large crowds. Galen's skill, influence, and self-confidence helped him become the leader of Roman physicians.

Galen wrote 500 medical books filled with detailed information about his experiences treating patients and his theories about disease. In *On Parts Affected by Disease*, Galen provides an organ-by-organ description of disease. Another important book, *The Uses of the Parts of the Body of Man*, concentrated on anatomy and *physiology*. Anatomy is the study of the body's internal structures, and physiology is the study of how these parts work together. Because the book describes studies of living animals, Galen is considered the founder of experimental physiology.

The Uses of the Parts of the Body of Man includes information about the function of the heart, brain, nerves, and kidneys. It explains how nerves control breathing and that urine is produced by the kidneys. It even provides evidence for Rufus's idea that the heart pumps blood through the arteries. This text was used by European doctors until well into the 1500s.

When Galen died, Rome lost its most important medical leader, and Roman medicine gradually returned to its old ways. Instead of approaching medicine as a science, it was viewed as a type of magic. Healers relied on potions of camel's brains or turtle's blood to cure some conditions. Romans routinely made sacrifices to Scabies, the goddess of the itch, and to Febris, the goddess of fever.

chapter5
How the Romans Measured Time

III

XCV

A sundial

Few Romans were interested in astronomy. They did not concern themselves with questions like "What is Earth's place in the universe?" or "How do the planets move?" They were more interested in developing practical uses for astronomy. This included finding better ways to measure time—the time of day and the time of year.

The Time of Day

Among the treasures that victorious Roman legions brought back from the conquered town of Cantania, which was on the island of Sicily, was a *sundial*. A sundial is the oldest known device for measuring time. It consists of a dial face, which is divided into hours, and a pointer, a flat piece of metal set in the center of the dial. When sunlight hits the pointer, also called a *gnomon*, the light casts a shadow that indicates the time.

The Romans installed this sundial in the Forum in the center of Rome about 2,300 years ago. For 100 years, Romans passed it every day, never realizing that it gave the wrong time. In order for a sundial to tell the correct time, the upper edge of the pointer must slant upward from the dial face at an angle equal to the *latitude* of the location of the sundial. It never occurred to the Romans that a sundial built to serve a town 330 miles (530 km) to the southeast could not accurately measure time in the city of Rome. Eventually, Romans studying Greek writings learned that the sundial's pointer needed to be adjusted for it to show the correct time.

Improving the Calendar

For centuries, Romans used the phases of the moon to measure the passage of time. According to their lunar calendars, each new moon marked the first day of a new month. Each new year began when 10 months had passed. As a result, their year was just 304 days long. Eventually, the ruler Numa Pompilius added two more months to the calendar to create a year that had 355 days.

Today, our months do not coincide exactly with the phases of the moon. We know that a lunar cycle is about 28 days, but most months are 30 or 31 days long. This gives us a year that is about 365 days long. Because the early Romans had shorter months, they also had shorter years.

This 10-day difference may not seem like such a big deal, but think about it. If every year was 10 days shorter, there would come a time when May would fall during the late summer and September would be in the middle of winter.

This type of calendar was useless to Roman farmers. They needed a calendar that would

The Romans began each month on the first night a new crescent moon was seen.

Numa Pompilius, an early Roman ruler, who revised the calendar

let them know when they should plant and harvest their crops. They wanted to know when they could expect spring, summer, winter, and autumn weather. Rather than use the inaccurate Roman calendar, Roman farmers used the positions of the stars to plan their planting schedules. So, as farmers turned to the heavens for guidance, the rest of Rome continued to use their flawed calendar.

All this changed about 2,000 years ago. Each year, the Romans celebrated the beginning of spring with a festival called Floralia. When that day fell in the middle of summer, Roman emperor Julius Caesar decided something had to be done about the calendar. Caesar consulted a Greek astronomer named Sosigenes.

Sosigenes advised that the Roman calendar be based on the sun, rather than the moon. A solar calender would have 365 days, instead of 355 days. Sosigenes also recommended that an extra day be added to the calendar every 4 years. This "leap year" would make the calendar year almost exactly equal to the amount of time it takes for Earth to revolve around the

Julius Caesar was one of Rome's greatest rulers.

A Julian calendar with months and days of the week marked with pegs

sun once. Caesar followed this advice and created the Julian calendar. In reality, the true length of a solar year is not exactly 365 ¼ days. It is 365.242199 days, or 365 days, 5 hours, 48 minutes and 46 seconds. This means that the Julian calender was about 11 minutes too long.

Again, this may not seem too significant. Over the course of centuries, however, it made a difference. Pope Gregory XIII eliminated 10 days from the year 1582 to correct for the error. The Gregorian calender is the one we use today.

A group of men gathered in Sienna, Italy to decide how such an error could be avoided in the future. Their solution was to change the leap year rule. Every fourth year would still be considered a leap year unless

How the Months Were Named

GREGORIAN MONTH	JULIAN MONTH	MEANING/ORIGIN
January	Januarius	Named after the Roman god Janus; Janus stood watch by the door of all Roman homes
February	Februarius	From the Latin word for "cleansing" or "purification"; the Roman feast of religious purification was held each year on February 15
March	Martius	Named after the Roman god Mars; the god of war
April	Aprilis	From the Latin word for "opening" because this is the month when flowers begin to bloom
May	Maius	From the Latin word for "growth"
June	Junius	From the Latin word for "ripening"
July	Julius	Named in honor of Julius Caesar
August	Augustus	Named in honor of Caesar Augustus, who ruled Rome after Julius Caesar
September	September	The name of the seventh month of the old Roman calendar; the prefix *sept-* means "seven" in Latin
October	October	The name of the eighth month of the old Roman calendar; the prefix *oct-* means "eight" in Latin
November	November	The name of the ninth month of the old Roman calendar; the prefix *nov-* means "nine" in Latin
December	December	The name of the tenth month of the old Roman calendar; the prefix *dec-* means "ten" in Latin

it ended in 00 (1600, 1700, 1800). These years would only be leap years if they could be divided by 400. As a result, 1600 was a leap year, but 1700, 1800, and 1900 were not. The year 2000 will be a leap year.

Besides giving all of Rome, and farmers in particular, a truly useful calendar, Caesar also developed a kind of farmer's almanac. His book, *De Astris*, provided instructions for using the positions of the stars and planets to predict the weather of the upcoming year.

In 1582, a group of prominent men gathered in Sienna, Italy, to discuss reforming the calender.

chapter 6
The Roman Legacy

III

XCVI

This depiction of life in ancient
Rome was painted around 1500.

Even though the Romans were not interested in studying science for the sake of gaining knowledge, they should be remembered as the civilization that took information accumulated by Egypt and Greece and used it to build great buildings, develop an extremely accurate calendar, and preserve the health of its citizens.

For centuries, engineers relied on the writings of the Roman aqueduct designer Frontinus for guidance in building water-supply systems.

One of Frontius's sketches of a water-supply system

The Romans were the first to understand the importance of inspecting food and exercising in gymnasiums to maintain physical health. They were also the first to have military hospitals, medical insurance, medical schools, and licensing exams for doctors.

In 1842, when a British commission was appointed to find ways to improve the health of London's people, they developed a sewer system modeled after those built by the Romans.

The Romans are also credited with inventing a wide assortment of useful items—staircases, window-panes, milestone roadmarkers, keys, bellows with a nozzle, and such tools as the brace and bit, scissors, the borer, and the punch.

While building their great roads and seaports, they developed better ways to survey land. They were also the first people to cultivate oysters and plant fruit trees in orchards.

A Roman milestone built about 2,200 years ago

After the Fall of Rome

The Roman Empire was finally defeated by Germanic peoples in 476. That year marked more than the end of one of the world's greatest civilizations. It also marked the end of the ancient world and the beginning of a period known as Medieval Times or the Dark Ages. Historians call this period the Dark Ages because people seemed to lose interest in learning. In other words, the "light" of seeking knowledge went out during that time.

Europe was divided into many small kingdoms and estates. Each was governed by its own king or noble. These rulers spent their time fighting each other for land and possessions. By the early 1300s, the land we now call Italy was divided into 250 separate states.

While kings and nobles battled, the common people, who were poor and uneducated, farmed the land and gave most of their harvest to their lord. Very few people spent time studying ancient texts or

A calendar depicting Medieval life in Europe

observing the world around them. For nearly 1,000 years, Europe made little intellectual or technical progress. Rome's beautiful domed buildings and gracefully arched aqueducts fell into ruin. People went back to living in thatched huts and bathing in the river.

Among those who continued to care about learning, philosophy, and science was Roman historian Martianus Capella, who lived during the 500s. He collected ancient texts describing geometry, geography, astronomy, and mathematics. Boethius and Cassiodorus, who lived around the same time as Capella, copied and summarized the work of great thinkers including Euclid, a mathematician, and Ptolemy, an astronomer. Fortunately, these writings were preserved throughout the Dark Ages.

In the late 1300s and early 1400s, scientists and philosophers rediscovered the writings of Capella, Boethius, and Cassiodorus. They also read ancient texts that had been collected and preserved by the Muslims. These documents spurred the new interest in science and scientific discovery that characterized the period called the *Renaissance*. That same scientific spirit has been carried across time and continues to inspire us today.

Roman philosopher and statesman Anicius Manlius Severinus Boethius

GLOSSARY

alchemist—someone who searched for ways to extend life and turn common metals into gold.

amputate—to remove by cutting. Limbs with life-threatening bacterial infections are sometimes amputated.

anatomy—the study of an organism's body structure.

aqueduct—a channel for carrying water. In Roman times, aqueducts were made of concrete and supported by tall arches.

artery—a vessel that carries blood from the heart to other parts of the body.

barrel vault (tunnel vault)—a long thick concrete arch shaped like half a barrel.

cataract—a clouding of the lens of the eye that prevents light from passing through and impairs vision.

civilization—the culture of people living in a particular area during a specific period of time.

compost—a mixture of decayed organic matter and soil that makes excellent fertilizer.

concrete—a mixture of powdered lime and water to which sand and stone is added.

contagious—transmitted by physical contact.

cross vault (groin vault)—two barrel vaults that intersect at right angles. A cross vault allows natural light to enter a building.

diabetes—a medical condition in which the body fails to use sugar properly.

diagnose—to identify a particular medical condition by its symptoms.

gnomon—the pointer on a sundial.

latitude—the angular distance north or south of the equator.

leprosy—a chronic disease caused by a bacterial infection.

malaria—a disease that produces chills and fever, transmitted by the bite of a certain kind of mosquito.

nitrogen—a gas that makes up about 78 percent of Earth's atmosphere.

ore—a mineral that is mined because it contains a useful material, such as a metal.

organic—derived from or relating to a living organism.

physiology—the study of an organism's body functions.

Renaissance—literally, rebirth; the years from the 1300s to the 1600s in Europe, marked by a renewed interest in art, literature, and science.

smelt—to melt or fuse, often in order to bring about a chemical change.

sundial—an instrument that shows the time of day based on a shadow cast by a vertical pointer called a gnomon.

RESOURCES

Books

Boorstin, Daniel J. *The Discoverers.* New York: Random House,1983.

Clark, Ronald W. *Works of Man.* New York: Viking, 1985.

Ganeri, Anita. *How Would You Survive as an Ancient Roman?* London: Watts, 1995.

Hill, Donald. *A History of Engineering in Classical and Medieval Times.* La Salle, IL: Open Court, 1984.

Kerr, Daisy. *Ancient Romans.* London: Watts, 1996.

Ronan, Colin A. *Science: Its History and Development.* New York: Facts on File, 1982.

Starr, Chester G. *A History of the Ancient World.* London: Oxford, 1983.

Internet Sites

Due to the changeable nature of the Internet, sites appear and disappear very quickly. The following resources offered useful information on ancient Rome at the time of publication.

Exploring Ancient World Culture includes maps, timelines, essays, and images that describe ancient civilizations in India, Rome, Greece, and the Near East. It can be reached at **http://eawc.evansville.edu/index.htm**.

East Middle School's Ancient Culture Page provides information about many of the world's ancient civilizations. You can learn about the ancient Greeks, Romans, Chinese, and Mayans at **http://www.macatawa.org/org/ems/anccult.html**.

Ancient World Web provides descriptions of many web sites that have information about ancient civilizations. Its address is **http://atlantic.evsc.virginia.edu/julia/AncientWorld.html**.

INDEX

ABOUT THE AUTHOR

Jacqueline L. Harris is the author of ten books for young people, including *Nine Black American Doctors, Communicable Diseases, Learning Disorders, Drugs and Disease, Hereditary Diseases*, and *Henry Ford*. She has also contributed to a set of science readers and an encyclopedia of the environment. She has been a science editor for *Current Science* and *New Book of Knowledge* as well as a medical writer for a pharmaceutical company.

Harris earned a Bachelor of Science in bacteriology/chemistry from Ohio State University. Following an internship in medical technology, she worked as a clinical chemist and bacteriologist. She served two tours on the hospital ship S.S. *Hope* in Peru and Ecuador, teaching clinical laboratory procedures. Returning from the *Hope*, Harris went back to Ohio State to earn a degree in journalism. A career in science and medical writing followed.